CRAZY PETS

Ripley's
Believe It or Not!®
Kids

& CUTE ANIMALS

Consultant Camilla de la Bedoyere
Design Michelle Foster
Reprographics Juice Creative

ISBN 978-1-60991-120-1

For information regarding permission, write to
VP Intellectual Property
Ripley Entertainment Inc.
Suite 188, 7576 Kingspointe Parkway
Orlando, Florida, 32819, USA
Email: publishing@ripleys.com

Manufactured in China
in October/2014
1st printing

Library of Congress Control Number: 2014952893

PUBLISHER'S NOTE
While every effort has been made to verify the
accuracy of the entries in this book, the Publishers
cannot be held responsible for any errors contained
in the work. They would be glad to receive any
information from readers.

WARNING
Some of the stunts and activities in this book
are undertaken by experts and should not be
attempted by anyone without adequate training
and supervision.

www.ripleys.com/books

CRAZY PETS

Ripley's
Believe It or Not!
Kids
& CUTE ANIMALS

RIPLEY
PUBLISHING

a Jim Pattison Company

Babies on Board

Go faster!
Go faster!

Grebe chicks travel on their parents' back after hatching.

Can dogs ride horses?

Hiya!

Yes! Hekan, a border collie, rides and helps his owner Steve Jefferys to train horses.

A newborn ferret is so small it can fit into a teaspoon.

BUNNY FACTS

A rabbit's teeth never stop growing.

When rabbits jump and twist out of excitement, it's called a binky.

Rabbits can sleep with their eyes open.

Rabbits' ears can be as long as 4 inches (10 cm).

Rabbits can jump up to 3 feet (1 m) high.

Baby bunnies are called kits, which is short for kitten.

See Darius the world's largest rabbit on page 113!

Rabbits' noses twitch 20 to 120 times a minute.

They twitch faster when excited or stressed and slower when relaxed or sleeping.

CUTE
AND CUDDLY

Four tiny tawny owls were taken under the wing of a cuddly-toy mother! When the babies were left on their own, this stuffed owl took on the role. They love to snuggle up to her!

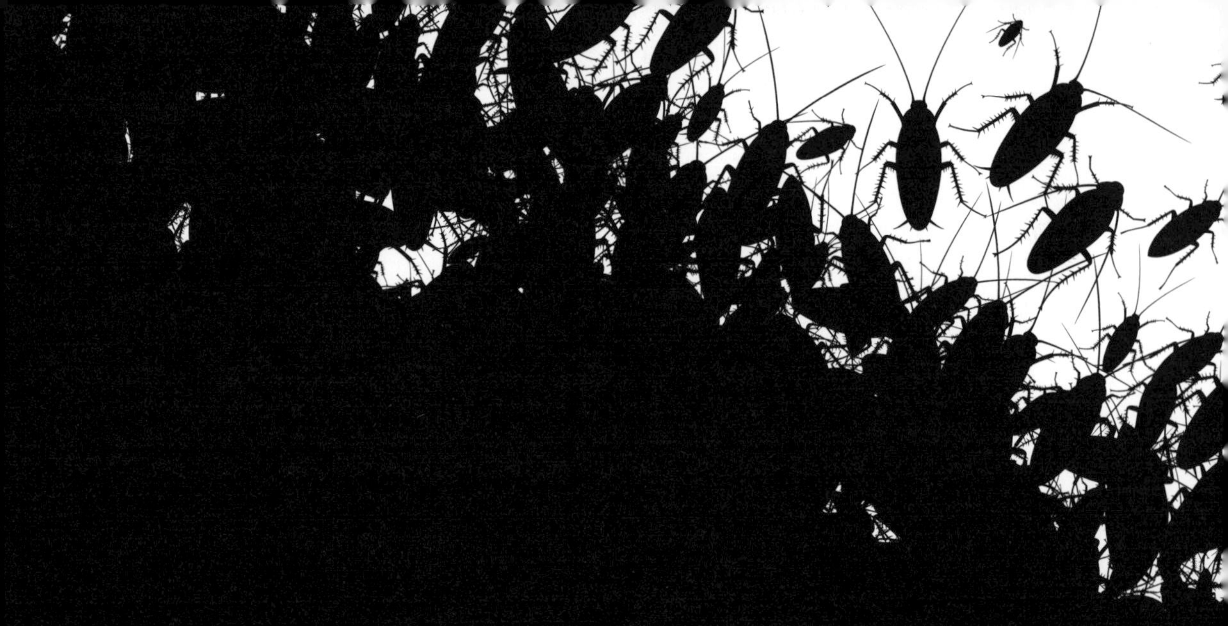

A man in China kept
200,000
creepy-crawly
cockroaches
as pets!

A pair of chameleons named Charles and Camilla had 56 babies!

Chameleons change color depending on their mood.

Ow!

Watch it Liz!

TINY DOGS

The world's smallest dog breed is the Chihuahua.

It's not easy being this cute.

Tiger the cat
had 27 toes!

That's a record!

TOILET TANK

You can fish and flush at the same time on this aquarium toilet! The fish don't actually share a tank with the toilet so you can't flush them away. Phew!

Karen Ferrier is Dalmatian mad! She loves anything that is black-and-white and spotty, and has over 3,500 items in her collection, including her dog named Ditto!

SPOT THE DOG

SOME PARROTS LOVE DANCING TO POP MUSIC!

You put your left claw up...

The smallest adult cat ever was called Tinker Toy...

weight = 1 pound 8 ounces (660 g)

height = $2\frac{3}{4}$ inches (7 cm)

length = $7\frac{1}{2}$ inches (19 cm)

A newborn kangaroo is only 1 inch (2.5 cm) long.

That's about the same size as this grape!

AMAZING ANIMALS

BOUNCY DOG!

A Staffordshire bull terrier called Harvey used a child's trampoline to bounce right out of his owner's yard in England. Harvey bounced into the neighbor's yard, ran away and was found four days later unharmed.

SURPRISE CAT!

When Mary Martell arrived at her hotel in Ontario, Canada, after flying from New Brunswick, Canada, she opened her suitcase and was surprised to find her cat Ginger! He had jumped inside the case when she was packing!

UNUSUAL BRIDESMAID!

When Renee Biwer married Terry Morris in August 2006 they had an unusual bridesmaid—Henrietta the hen! The clucky lady had been the groom's favorite pet for 12 years.

23

Most cats don't have eyelashes.

Rabbits eat their own droppings!

Any ketchup with that?

18,113 dogs

took part in the

largest ever

dog walk in the U.K. in 2010!

Here boy!

Babe's Island

Babe the wild boar lives on his own private island in The Bahamas... well, nearly. He actually shares it with two humans who feed and look after him. He loves the beach and taking strolls along the shore!

GAME, SET, MUTT...

These sporty dogs helped celebrate the launch of a new dog food in the U.K. by trying out rackets and balls!

29

Mini Me!

Hercules the miniature pony,
who is just 26 inches (66 cm) tall,
loves playing with his
even smaller friend
Penny, an African
Pigmy goat.

Chase me!!

Rats can hold
their breath
for up to
**three
minutes**
underwater.

Dogs

have lived with
humans for

30,000

years.

Scientists
believe that
dogs can
understand
human
feelings.

Cats have lived with humans for 5,000 years.

WHAT A JOKE!

What does a cat like to eat on a hot day?

A mice cream cone!

DOGGY DESSERT

Dr. Pro is an ice-cream parlor for dogs in Taiwan!

The dessert comes with a dog figure and dog biscuits.

Cats will **headbutt** you to show their **affection.**

Ouch! That hurt!

Who said that?

Hamsters can only see up to 6 inches (15 cm) in front of them.

KISSY KISSY!

Rob the giant rabbit and Chino the mini pig love to kiss and cuddle at Pennywell Farm, England.

100% CUTE!

Geckos' feet are VERY STICKY!

They are so sticky that they can hang from the ceiling by just one toe!

TOP 5
EXTREME PETS!

Jack's ears are so long they drag on the ground when he walks!

1. **LONG DOG EARS!** Jack the basset hound's ears are a massive 13 inches (33 cm) long!

2. **LONG DOG TONGUE!** Puggy the Pekingese has a 4.5-inch (11-cm) tongue.

3. **LONG CAT WHISKERS!** Whiskers has 12-inch (30-cm) long whiskers! That's as long as a ruler!

4. **OLD DOG!** Bluey the Australian cattle-dog lived to be 29 years 5 months old!

5. **OLD CAT!** Lucy the cat lived to be 39 years old!

DOG FACTS

There are over 84 million pet dogs in the U.S.A. That's more than in any other country in the world!

Until 2014, it was against the law to keep dogs as pets in Iceland.

Max, Bella, Bailey and Lucy are the most popular dog names.

There are around 400 million dogs in the world!

Dalmatians are born with normal hearing but about one in three Dalmatian puppies become deaf in at least one ear.

See the smallest puppy in the world on **page 151!**

Greyhounds are the fastest dogs. They can run up to 43 mph (69 km/h)!

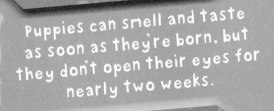

Puppies can smell and taste as soon as they're born, but they don't open their eyes for nearly two weeks.

BEST BUFFALO!

100% CRAZY!

When Sherron and R.C. Bridges renewed their wedding vows, guess who was the best man—their pet buffalo Wildthing!

SHOER

Pet snails can live to be 20 years old!

Chickens wash themselves with dust rather than water.

I need a shower!

BATMAN!

Steve Parker lives with his pet bat Nikki at his home in England. Nikki helps Steve to teach other people how to look after bats.

Hamsters' heads can triple in size

when their cheek pouches are full of food!

Greedy!

Some female hamsters stuff their babies into their cheek pouches to protect them.

Funny Face!

This fancy fish took part in the Goldfish & Fancy Carp Championship held in China in 2012. The contest features more than 1,000 fish every year.

Mother orangutans build a new home for their babies every night.

100% CUTE!

The heaviest hog in history was named Big Bill and weighed **2,552 pounds (1,157 kg)!**

That's the same weight as a small car!

WHAT A JOKE!

What do you call a pig with three eyes?

A piiig!

FIRST CLASS

A hamster nicknamed "Postie" survived being sent in the mail! Mailman Robert Maher spotted something wriggling inside an envelope and rescued the little creature.

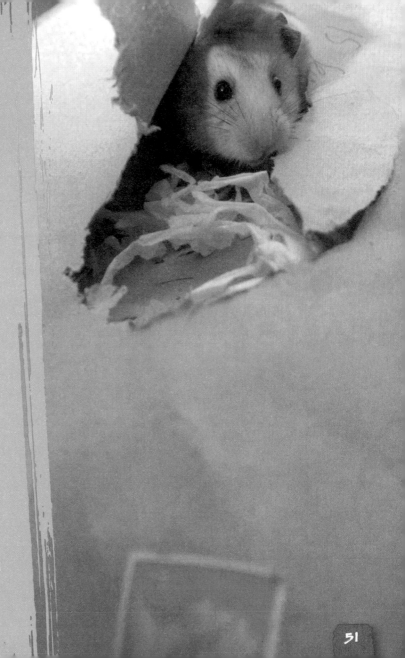

CRAZY CREATURES

EXTRA TOE!

The Russian blue breed of cat often has an extra toe on one of its paws.

DOGGY TRAVELS!

A Chihuahua traveled unharmed from Spain to Ireland inside a suitcase! The tiny dog was discovered by airport security in Ireland, after they thought it was a toy!

Peter Ash, from England, invented a device that hooked up his cell phone to the exercise wheel of his hamster to charge the phone. After the hamster had run for two minutes, Peter had 30 minutes of battery life!

PET TURTLE!

A man from China smuggled his pet turtle onto an airplane by fastening it to his back and pretending to have a hunchback!

A DAY IN THE LIFE OF Mr. Lee

What do cats do all day? Mr. Lee's owners wanted to find out, so they hung a little camera around his neck. The "cat cam" takes a picture every few minutes so they could follow his cat adventures.

What shall I do today?

Baby horses can stand up almost as soon as they are born.

Sheep were kept on the White House lawn when Woodrow Wilson was U.S. president.

HURDLING
HOGS

Miniature piglets jump over hurdles and other obstacles in races at Pennywell Farm in Devon, England.

Parakeets have three eyelids.

Mice are very good swimmers.

PANDA-PUPS

Aww! Look at these baby pandas play. But, look closer.... They're actually dogs painted to look like pandas at a pet park in China!

GLAMOR WOOF

These over-the-top dogs were snapped at fancy doggie events in New York by photographer Amy Lombard for her project "Doggies and Tiaras."

Aspen the Chihuahua looks glamorous at a beauty pageant.

At another doggy event, Valentino, a Pomeranian, is dressed as a hot dog!

Baa-lieve It or Not!

Nell Johnson from Australia has a pet sheep called Tiny Tot! She takes him for walks and he loves the attention.

Here, doggy!

Baaa, do I look like a dog?!

100% CRAZY!

Bluey the dog
lived to be
**29 years
5 months old!**
That's more
than 160
years old in
human years.

TOP 10
MOST POPULAR PETS IN THE U.S.A.

1. Dog
2. Cat
3. Hamster
4. Fish
5. Mouse
6. Guinea pig
7. Bird
8. Snake
9. Iguana
10. Ferret

If humans varied in size as much as dogs, the tallest would be up to...

31 feet (9.4 m)

and the smallest...

2 feet (0.6 m)

A group of cats is called a glaring.

Spoon Fed

This orphaned chick was fed by a trash picker until big enough to be released back into the wild.

In the U.S.A.

50% of owners sleep with their cats...

...and...

...50% of owners sleep with their dogs.

In Ancient Egypt killing a cat was a **crime punishable by death.**

Goldfish don't have a stomach.

No wonder I'm hungry!

DOGGY STAR!

Chloe is a big star! She has been on the front page of fashion magazines, in music videos, and earns up to $900 a day!

Cats almost never meow at other cats...
only at humans.

A goat's eyes have rectangular pupils.

Think I've been watching too much TV!

Bite-sized Baby

This tiny baby squirrel was left without any family after thunderstorms hit New Delhi, India. A passerby rescued the little guy and fed him cherries.

100% CUTE!

HORSE FACTS

There are about 58 million horses in the world.

There were no horses in Australia until 1788.

The oldest horse that ever lived was 62 years old!

You can tell a horse's age by looking at its teeth.

Horses like sweet flavors and will usually spit out anything sour or bitter.

See Princess the hungry horse on page 120!

Horses' teeth take up more space in their head than their brain.

BIG BABY

Wayne Muller adopted this baby giraffe and named him "Baby X" after the giraffe's mother rejected him. Wayne will look after Baby X for five or six months until he can care for himself.

Look mom, I'm nearly as tall as you!

At just five days old Baby X is almost as tall as his new mom!

You're my best friend!

100% CUTE!

Paddle Pop the Maltese puppy and Angus the parakeet are best buddies! Angus rides around on Paddle Pop's back and whistles for the dog's attention when he's bored!

They even button-up underneath!

WINTER WARMERS

It's not everyday you see ponies in sweaters! These Shetland ponies look very cozy in their custom knits.

Up, up, and away...

A French puss named Felicette was the first cat in space! She was blasted into outer space in 1963 and, after a short mission, returned safely to Earth.

Hamsters' teeth never stop growing.

DO GOATS HAVE ACCENTS?

G'day mate!

'Ello mate!

Yes, they sound different in different parts of the world!

Howdy cowboy!

BIZARRE BEASTS

SHOPPING DOG!

A dog named Hello can shop by herself! She chooses the food, waits in line, hands over the money and then walks back to her home in Taiwan with the goods!

GETAWAY GOLDFISH!

Sparkle the goldfish survived seven hours out of his tank before being rescued. He had jumped out and was found on the carpet covered in fluff, but was returned safely to his tank!

PET SHARK!

Tom K. Maunupau, from Honolulu, Hawaii, had a pet shark and took rides on its back!

FUR BALLS!

Jeff the cat has so much fur that after he was groomed there was enough to make a furry lookalike cat!

I'm Jeff who are you?

Jeff lookalike made from Jeff's fur!

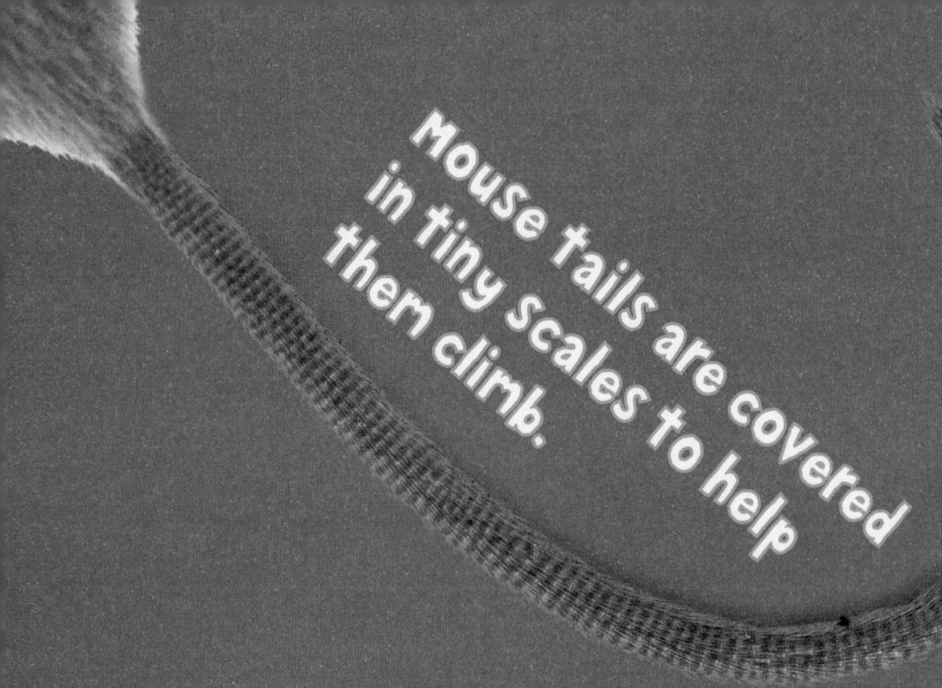

Mouse tails are covered in tiny scales to help them climb.

SOME BIRDS
EAT AT LEAST
HALF THEIR OWN WEIGHT
IN FOOD EACH DAY.

Prickly Situation

100% CUTE!

Norman the baby hedgehog lost one of his front teeth, and became an Internet sensation when his owner posted the picture online.

TOP 10

UNUSUAL

Read about Ripley's
Top 10 odd pets
in this book—
they're crazy!

Can grow to
3 inches (7 cm)
long!

ACTUAL
SIZE

Cockroach

PETS

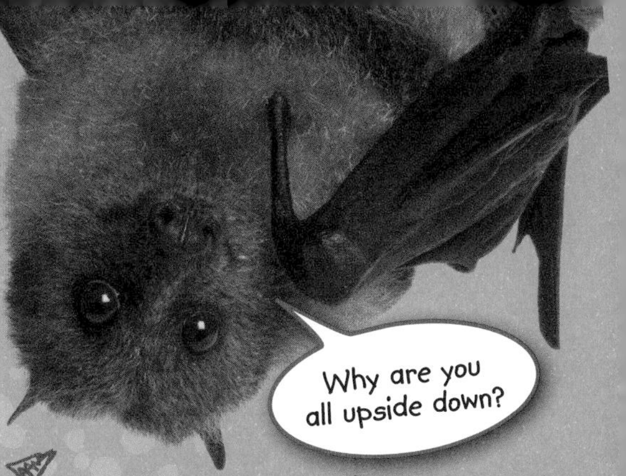

Why are you all upside down?
Bat

100% CRAZY!

6 Bat page 45

7 Hedgehog page 89

8 Donkey page 147

9 Chameleon page 13

10 Capybara (related to the guinea pig) page 148

Hedgehog

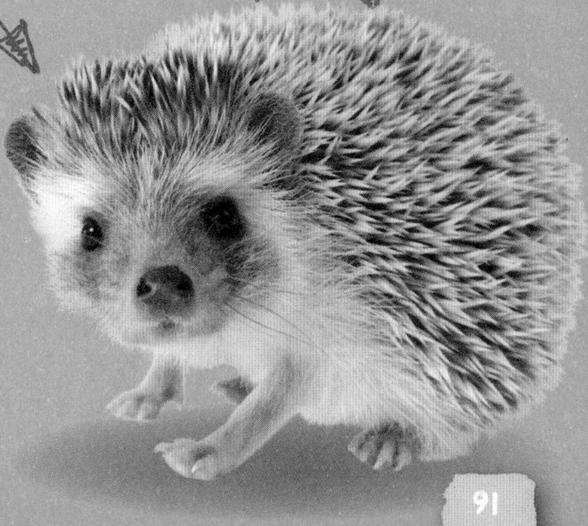

smile!

Newborn pandas are about the size of an apple!

These tiny fur balls are actually giant panda babies!

100% CUTE!

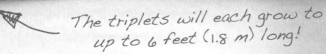
The triplets will each grow to up to 6 feet (1.8 m) long!

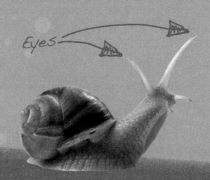

Eyes

A snail's eyes
are at the
end of its
longest pair
of tentacles.

SURF'S UP!

Surfing holds no fear for Boomer Hodel's star water rat. The rat even has its own custom-made foot-long surfboard.

Weeeeeee!

Buddy the dog loves to fly! He has flown in a paraglider over 75 times in his doggy harness, with his owner Bill.

100% CRAZY!

Buddy! Where are you?

DO all dogs bark?

No, the basenji is the world's only barkless dog. It makes a yodeling noise instead!

Pigs enjoy listening to music.

BATLAMB!

Kapow!

A baby sheep in Norway was named Batlamb after it was born with a furry superhero-like pattern on its face!

A rabbit's ears can turn in every direction.

Mice have 150 babies a year.

When rats smell cats their blood pressure shoots up...

even if they have never come across a real cat before!

A pet snake in Australia swallowed four golf balls thinking they were chicken eggs! The balls were removed and the snake survived.

VOTE FOR STEFANO!

Meglio un can
Politico
che un Polit
cane!

Stefano the dog is a political pooch! He was a candidate for a political party in Italy in 2012. Sadly, he didn't win.

I promise free bones!

Chinchillas don't have body odor.

Even their droppings don't smell for several days.

Snails don't have ears.

CURLY COAT

Believe it or not, this cuddly creature isn't a woolly sheep—it's a pig! The rare Mangalitsa pig has a curly coat with a piggy snout!

The short, stubby tail of a rabbit is known as a scut.

GOLDFISH
can't close their eyes.

They have no eyelids, so they have to sleep with their eyes open.

Zzzzzzz!

Some pigs are afraid of mud!

All kittens and puppies are born with blue eyes!

Parakeets poop 40 to 50 times a day!

Over half of all pet owners would rather be **stranded on a desert island with their pets** than with another person.

FARM FRIENDS

Love ya Billy!

Most goats can climb trees!

Goats are great companions for other farm animals, such as horses, cows and chickens.

TOP 6
BIG PETS

1. **Giant George the dog** is 3½ feet (1 m) tall.

2. **Ulric the cat** weighs 30 pounds (14 kg).

3. **Goldie the goldfish** is 15 inches (40 cm) long.

4. **Sammy the tortoise** weighs 115 pounds (52 kg).

5. **Gary the capybara** (looks like a big guinea pig) weighs 112 pounds (50 kg).

6. **Darius the rabbit** is 4 feet 4 inches (1.3 m) long.

DARIUS
the Giant Rabbit

Darius weighs 49 pounds
(22 kg) and measures
4 feet 4 inches (1.3 m),
making him the world's
biggest rabbit!

Darius
eats more
than 4,000
carrots
a year!

CAT FACTS

There are over 500 million pet cats in the world.

Cats can sleep for up to 18 hours a day!

Cats communicate by peeing on trees, fences and furniture!

A female cat is called a queen or a molly. A male is called a tomcat.

A cat uses its whiskers to test if it can squeeze through a small space.

A cat's front paws have five toes, the back paws have four.

Cats often flick their tails to show they are not happy.

See The Rock Cats on page 158!

PIGS IN PAINT!

Miniature pigs Del Boy and Rodney made the news with their unusual paintings. They dipped their snouts and trotters in children's finger paint and rolled around on a canvas to create their art!

What do they call you?

Pigasso!

WHAT A JOKE!
What do pigs write secret messages with? Invisible oink!

117

WACKY WILDLIFE

PERFORMING POODLE!

Chanda-Leah the performing poodle from Ontario, Canada, toured America with her owner Sharon Robinson showing audiences over 1,000 tricks. She could untie shoelaces, play the piano and even sort mail!

PIANO PUSS!

Nora the cat can play the piano with her paws! She has her own CD, DVD and downloadable ringtone.

HMMM... TASTY!

Edwin Rose from England has a very odd job—she tests cat and dog food by tasting it!

PET SNAIL!

Yang Jinsen from China had a pet snail that he took for walks and played with! With his love and care the pet lived for 11 years—twice as long as snails usually do.

HUNGRY HORSE!

Carissa Boulden's pet horse Princess enjoys eating every meal at the table at home in Sydney, Australia. Here she is slurping up some spaghetti bolognaise!

GIANT TORTOISES

can grow up to 5 feet (1.5 m) in length.

THAT'S LONGER THAN A BABY ELEPHANT!

Many hamsters only blink one eye at a time.

Dalmatians
have no
spots when
they are
born and are
completely
white!

TOP 10

Duckling →

CUTE BABY ANIMALS

1. Duckling
2. Hedgehog
3. Seal
4. Giant panda

5. Bunny
6. Elephant

Seal

7. Piglet

8. Kitten

9. Puppy

10. Lamb

WHAT A JOKE!

What do you call a pile of kittens? A meowntain!

Hedgehog

Giant panda

Elephant

Trailer PupS

The Pet Camper is perfect for animals that like to travel in style! The trailers can even be personally designed to suit your pet.

Chicks can talk to each other from inside their shells.

Morning James!

Morning Kyle!

Chicks use at least **24** different sounds to get to know each other before they hatch!

A pig's squeal

ranges from 110 to 115 decibels—that's nearly

as loud as a jumbo jet!

Tortoises can smell with their throats.

Stinkin' Cute

Eight-year-old Mimi has a very unusual pet—a skunk named Stoosh! Skunks are known for their stinky smell, which they release when they are in danger. Luckily, Stoosh has only ever sprayed her famous smell once— at the family's pet dog!

Stoosh follows Mimi around the house and even shares a bed with her.

Cats find it almost impossible to go down a tree head first.

Their curved claws are perfect for climbing up a tree, but not so good for getting down!

DO doGS
wear jewels?

Yes, sometimes!
You can buy a diamond
dog collar that costs
$3 million!

Some fish, like the triggerfish, can swim backward.

Snowball Monkeys

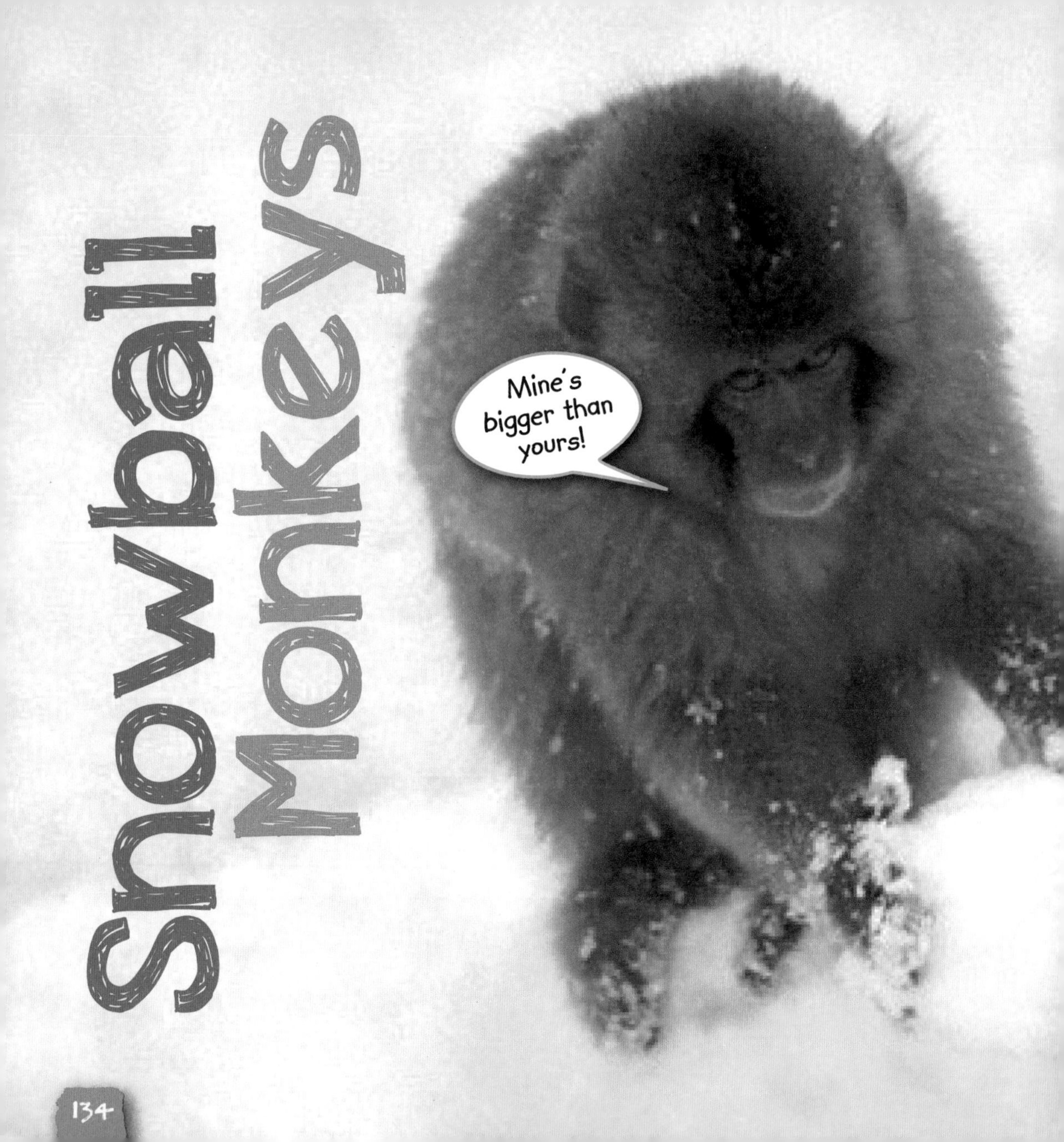

Young Japanese macaque
monkeys make snowballs for fun.

The wingspan of a hyacinth macaw is about the same as the height of an eight year old!

That's huge!

Xiaoyu the rabbit,
from China, is
addicted to TV!

She loves soap operas and attacks
her owners if they change the channel.

ME and ROO!

Left a bit, up a bit, mmm... perfect.

Julianne Bradley shares her home in Australia with Beemer her pet kangaroo! He eats at the table with her, plays football in the yard, and lives alongside Julianne's other pets—a sheep, three dogs and a cat!

When Beemer was rescued, he was so small Julianne kept him in a sock!

A pig's tongue has about **19,000** taste buds —that's about **10,000** more than a human.

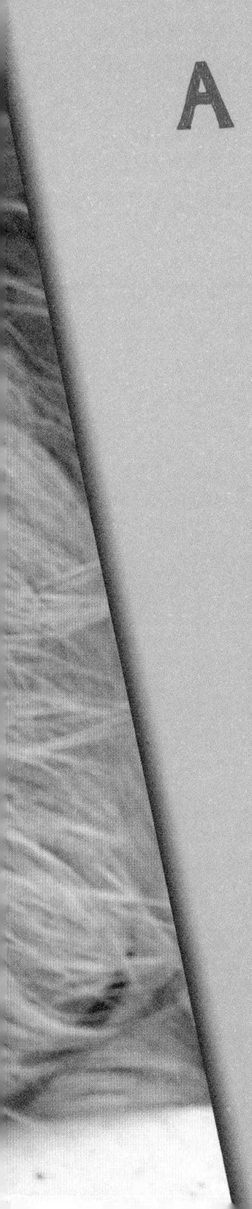

A cat can jump up
to five times its
own height in
a single leap.

IGUANAS ARE ABLE TO
HOLD THEIR BREATH FOR
UP TO 30 MINUTES.

There are over

300,000

snakes kept as pets in the U.K.

A goat's horns never stop growing.

Tail wagging has different meanings.

Dogs wag their tails more to the right when they're happy, and more to the left when they're nervous.

GOLDFISH FACTS

Goldfish are able to remember things for three months.

Some goldfish begin their life as a boy then turn into a girl— or the other way round!

Humans have been keeping goldfish as pets for over 2,000 years.

If you keep a goldfish in a dark room, it will lose some of its color.

Goldfish sometimes grow to over a foot (30 cm) long.

See what this fancy goldfish took part in on page 47!

Goldfish have been known to live for over 40 years!

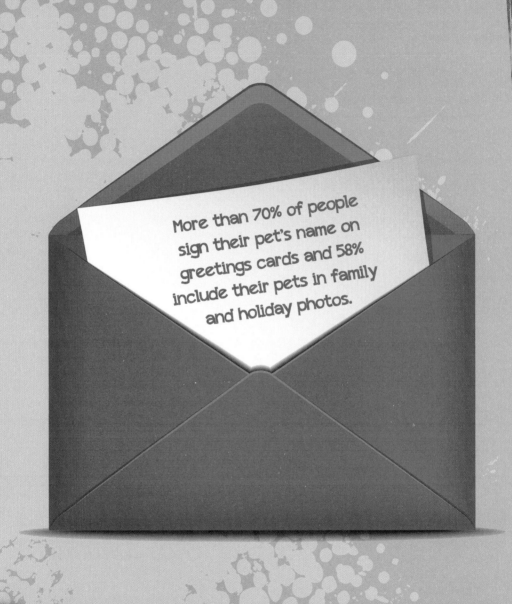

More than 70% of people sign their pet's name on greetings cards and 58% include their pets in family and holiday photos.

LONG LOCKS!

Nooooooooooo!

This hairy donkey is about to have a haircut for the first time in 17 years!

The rare Baudet du Poitou donkey is owned by Annie and Zoe Pollock from England.

ON THE ROAD!

Is it a dog? Is it a hamster? No, it's actually a capybara, a relative of the guinea pig AND the largest species of rodent in the world! Caplin Rous the capybara, who lives with owner Melanie Typaldos in Texas, loves traveling around in the back of the car.

About

500,000

Americans
own pet rats
or mice.

Mother pigs
"sing" to
their babies.

Smallest Puppy

Star the Chihuahua weighs less than 1 pound (0.5 kg). A normal Chihuahua weighs over 6 pounds!

100% CUTE!

AWESOME ANIMALS

HIGH FLYERS!

Did you know that dog fleas can jump higher than cat fleas?

READING DOG!

Willow the terrier can read up to 250 different words! Her trainer Lyssa Rosenberg, from New York, taught her to recognize words such as "sit" and "wave," and to perform actions.

Riana van Nieuwenhuizen, from South Africa, lives with three dogs, two wolves, three leopards, nine cheetahs, a lion and a jaguar! They share her kitchen and even her bed!

HOME ZOO!

PET REINDEER!

Gordon Elliot from London, England, has a pet reindeer called Dobey!

153

DOGS sometimes raise their left ear when meeting a stranger...

...and their right ear when they don't like something.

154

Mice need to eat 15 to 20 times a day.

Parakeets grind their beaks when they are **happy.**

Having a Ball!

Waffle the dog loves bringing balls home from her walks! She has found over 1,000 balls so far, including tennis balls, soccer balls and beach balls.

DO CATS ROCK?!

We rock!

Yes they do! Meet The Rock Cats, a real live rock band! These musical kitties have been taught to play instruments by their owner Samantha Martin from Texas. Cats really do rock!

159

Chinchillas can sleep hanging **UPSIDE DOWN** **UPRIGHT** ...or **ON THEIR SIDES.**

Awwwwww!

Turtles can't stick their tongues out.

Americans spend about

$56 billion

on their pets every year.

A cat's heart beats about twice as fast as yours.

John Huntington from Sydney, Australia, has a pet chicken called Goldie! He takes her for walks in the city.

Skiing Squirrel

Twiggy the squirrel can waterski! He rides his tiny skis around a heated pool.

Squirrels can run up to 20 mph (30 km/h).

Hedgehogs can swim really well.

WHAT A JOKE!

What's a hedgehog's favorite flavor of crisps? Prickled onion!

The chicken is the closest living relative to the Tyrannosaurus rex.

Pigs communicate with each other using around 20 different noises.

Can parrots skate?

Yes they can—and bowl, and play basketball! The Cardoza family from California have taught their parrots how to really enjoy life!

MOP DOG

The hairy coats of Hungarian Komondor dogs twist into cords 8–11 inches (20–27 cm) long!

Anastasia the Jack Russell terrier popped 100 balloons in 44.49 seconds.

A HUG IN A MUG!

These four-day-old piglets weigh just 12 ounces (350 g) each! That's the same as a can of soup!

Piglets double in weight just seven days after birth.

100% CUTE!

TOP 4 RICH DOGS

1 GUNTHER IV THE GERMAN SHEPHERD WAS LEFT $372 MILLION.

2 TOBY RIMES THE POODLE WAS LEFT $80 MILLION.

3 TROUBLE THE MALTESE WAS LEFT $12 MILLION.

4 PONTIAC THE GOLDEN RETRIEVER WAS LEFT $5 MILLION.

You can buy sunglasses for your dog, called doggles, to match yours!

Canaries can sing
two songs
at the same time.

TORTOISE FACTS

A tortoise's shell is sensitive to touch.

Tortoises can be very noisy! The red-footed tortoise makes a sound like a chicken!

A group of tortoises is called a creep.

Tortoises can live to be over 100 years old.

Tortoises from hot countries often have lighter colored shells than those that live in cooler places.

Tortoises have ears inside their heads.

The fastest recorded tortoise speed is 5 mph (8 km/h).

Fashion PIG

Penelope the miniature pig loves dressing up! She has become an Internet sensation after her owners posted pictures of her on Instagram.

Like my hat?

177

DOGWATCH!

Bilbo, a Newfoundland, is Britain's first doggy lifeguard. Newfoundlands have webbed feet and a waterproof coat, which makes them great swimmers.

RESCUE

Penwith District Council

FESAVING NO

THE DESERT HAMSTER IS JUST 2 INCHES (5.5 CM) LONG.

ACTUAL SIZE!

IT WEIGHS JUST 1 OUNCE (30 G)!

Goldfish
can see more colors than humans can.

There are about **920** different breeds of cows in the world.

TOP 4
Petworking

Did you know that one in ten pets is on Facebook! These pets are some of the most famous "petworkers"...

1 **Maru the cat** from Japan loves playing in cardboard boxes and has over **200 million YouTube views.**

2 **Bizkit the dog** has been filmed sleepwalking and has over **37 million YouTube views.**

3 **Boo the dog** uploads a cute photo each day to Facebook and has over **15 million likes.**

4 **Sockington the cat** from Boston tweets his thoughts on Twitter and has over **1.3 million followers.**

Boo the Pomeranian dog gets pampered at a luxury hotel in Las Vegas.

Boo even has his own photo book called "Boo, the life of the world's cutest dog."

MP

183

BADGER BEDS!

These baby badgers were separated from their families after floods destroyed their homes in the U.K. Luckily, local people rescued the babies, and kept them safe and warm in these badger beds.

A badger eats hundreds of earthworms each night!

CRAZY CRITTERS

PET SCORPIONS!

Suang Puangsri from Thailand has 4,600 pet scorpions! He says he has been stung so often that he is immune to their poison.

OPERA DOG!

Judith Dodworth's pet greyhound Pikelet loves to sing opera! When Judith starts singing opera Pikelet can't help but join in!

LUCKY BIRDIES!

Carpenter John Looser from Toronto, Canada, creates mini mansions for birds. They cost up to $2,500, have up to 100 rooms, and can even include a swimming pool!

SLEEPY DOG!

The Leroy family, from Washington state, discovered that a stray dog had been sleeping in their car at night—it had been opening the doors by itself!

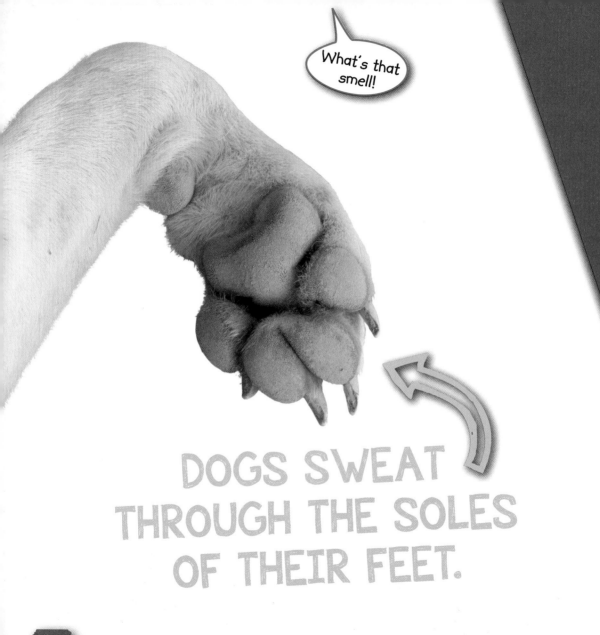

DOGS SWEAT THROUGH THE SOLES OF THEIR FEET.

Snails have tiny teeth on their tongues, which they use to scrape up food.

A BEEFALO
is part bison and part cow.

PINK CAT

Brumas the cat turned pink!
His owners have no idea
how or why it happened!

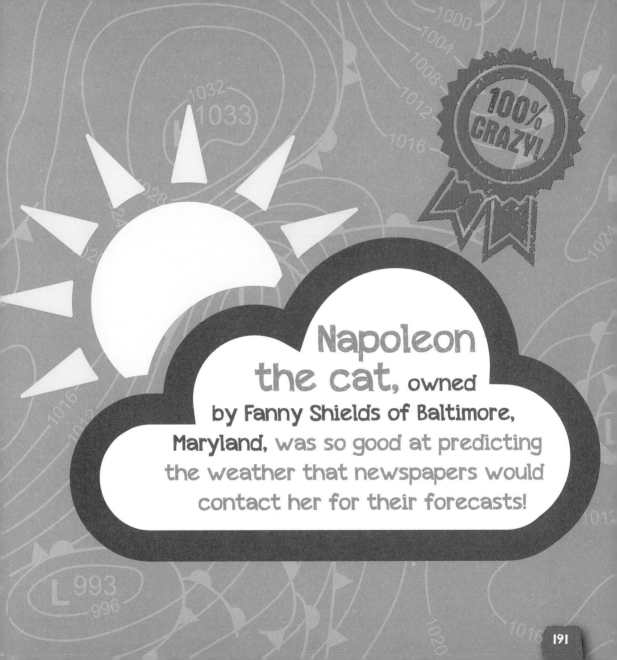

100% CRAZY!

Napoleon the cat, owned by Fanny Shields of Baltimore, Maryland, was so good at predicting the weather that newspapers would contact her for their forecasts!

SUPER SKILLS

Marisa Zilli is a very talented animal trainer from Ontario, Canada. She trains dogs, cats, ferrets and even rats to perform fun tricks!

Famous can dunk a basketball!

Shadow **can play soccer!**

Raven **can walk across a tightrope, whoa!**

Suki **can roll a spool!**

The most dogs ever owned by one person were

5,000 mastiffs

that belonged to 13th-century Mongol emperor Kublai Khan.

Female goats have beards, just like the males.

DO dogs dream?

zzzzzzzz!

Small dogs have more dreams than big dogs!

Zzzzzz...

zzzzzzzzzzz!

Yes!

They twitch and quiver in their sleep, which shows they dream just like us.

The closest relative to an elephant shrew **is an elephant** not a shrew.

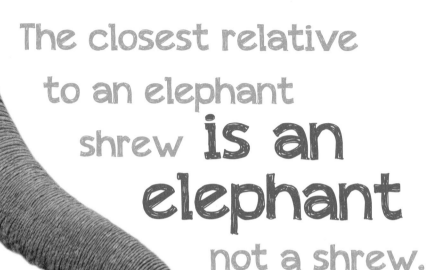

Hey cuz!

The shell of a tortoise is formed from 60 different bones that are all joined together.

Pigs can run 11 mph (17 km/h).

That's faster than a person running a six-minute mile!

LOOKING GOOD?

Ugly dog contests are held every year, and here you can meet some of the most adorably ugly competitors....

Peanut

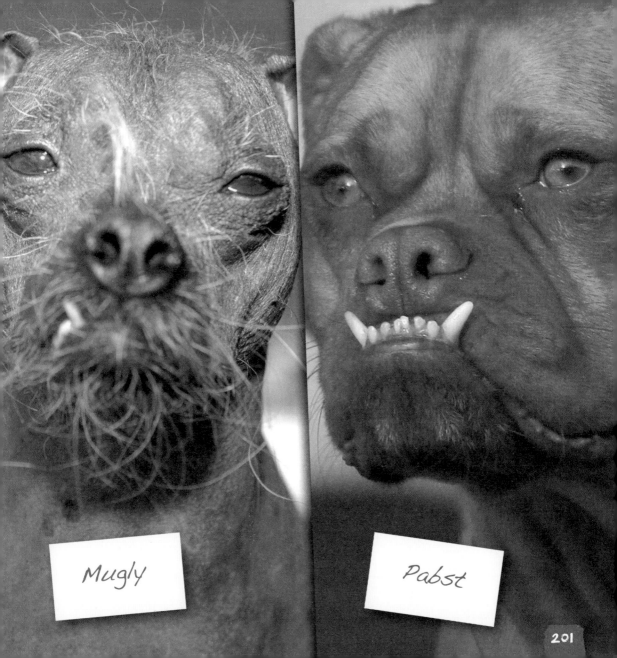

Mugly

Pabst

A dog's nose has a unique set of lines and ridges, just like a human fingerprint.

25% OF AMERICAN PET OWNERS BLOW-DRY THEIR PET.

Mice can squeeze through a tiny **0.2 inch (6 mm)** gap.

GIANT Goldfish

What do they feed him?!

Bruce the goldfish measures over 17 inches (43 cm) long. Here he is swimming in his tank with regular-sized goldfish friends.

When I grow up I want to be like Bruce!

Lucy the micro
Yorkshire terrier
is the world's
smallest
working dog!

Lucy works as a
therapy dog and is
just 5.7 inches
(14.5 cm) tall!

ACTUAL
SIZE!

Mice talk to each other.

They talk in mouse sounds that humans can't even hear.

The chow chow dog has a **blue-black tongue.**

Shall we call her Polly?

Parrots give their babies names.

Hamsters can be taught to come when their name is called.

House Horse

Nasar the horse found a new home inside his owners' house during a storm and won't leave! He stares at himself in the mirror, plays keyboard with his nose and has only broken one cup, so far!

Many fish can taste without opening their mouth. They have tastebuds all over their body.

A third of owners talk to their dogs

on the phone ...or leave messages on an answering machine!

Twice as many new dogs than babies arrive in U.S. homes every year.

Tea and... Cats!

The "Cat Café" in London, England, is home to 11 rescue cats who hang out with customers. The cats also have a private garden for when they want some me (ow) time!

PLEASE
WAIT
HERE UNTIL
YOU ARE
CALLED

THE 100%
CRAZY!

LADY DINAH'S
CAT EMPORIUM

LADY DINAH'S
CAT EMPORIUM

CARINGDONS

BIRD FACTS

Some parrot species can live for over 80 years.

The total weight of a bird's feathers is often more than its skeleton.

There are one million pet birds in the U.K.

Ducks' feathers are waterproof.

A special gland near the tail produces an oil that covers and protects their feathers.

See Angus the parakeet's best friend on page 78!

The most common bird on the planet is the chicken.

In some species, a bird's eye takes up 50% of its head. Our eyes take up just 5% of our head.

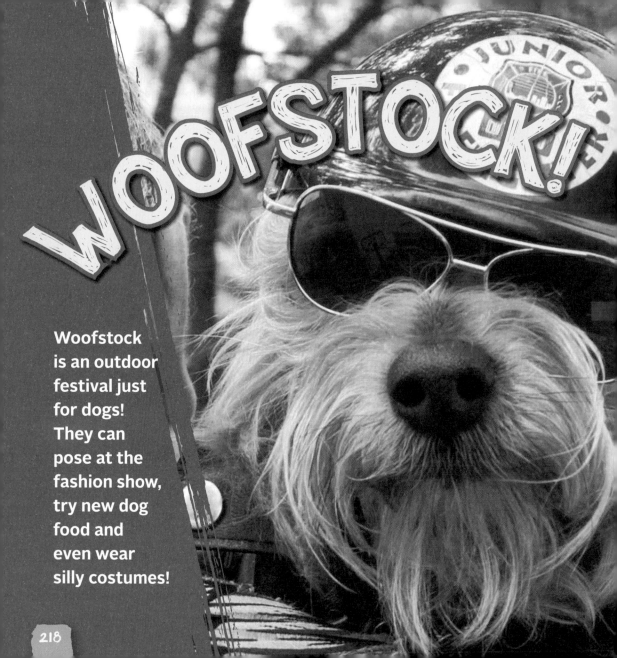

WOOFSTOCK!

Woofstock is an outdoor festival just for dogs! They can pose at the fashion show, try new dog food and even wear silly costumes!

218

INDEX

A
aquarium toilet 17

B
badgers 184–185
bats 45, 91
beefalos 189
birds 64, 88, 187, 216–217
  canaries 173
  chickens 23, 44, 110, 162, 165, 217
  chicks 6, 128
  ducks 124, 217
  grebes 4–5
  macaws 136
  owls 10–11
  parakeets 58, 109, 155
  parrots 20, 78–79, 166–167, 209, 216
bison 189
buffalos 42–43

C
capybaras 91, 112, 148–149
cats 35, 64, 66–67, 70, 114–115
  big cats 112
  café for 214–215
  camera on 54–55
  climbing trees 132
  domestication 33
  eyes 24, 108
  fur 86–87, 190
  hearts 162
  jumping 141
  lifespan 39
  meowing 72
  and music 118, 158–159
  online 182

cats (*cont.*)
  paws 16, 52, 115
  predict weather 191
  sleep 7, 114
  small cats 21
  in space 82
  in suitcase 23
  tails 115
  whiskers 39, 115
chameleons 13, 91
cheetahs 153
chinchillas 104, 160
cockroaches 12, 90
cows 181, 189

D
dinosaurs 165
dogs 25, 40–41, 64, 68, 71, 103, 126–127
  barking 98
  basenjis 98
  basset hounds 39
  big dogs 112
  bull terriers 22
  Chihuahuas 15, 53, 60–61, 151
  chow chows 208
  coats 168–169
  collects balls 156–157
  Dalmatians 18–19, 41, 123
  domestication 32
  dreams 196–197
  dressing up 28–29, 59, 60–61, 133, 173, 218–219
  ears 38–39, 41, 154
  eyes 41, 108
  on Facebook 182–183
  flying 96–97
  food 34
  German shepherds 172
  golden retrievers 172

dogs (*cont.*)
  greyhounds 41, 187
  Jack Russell terriers 170
  Komondors 168–169
  lifespan 39, 63
  Malteses 78–79, 172
  mastiffs 194
  names 40
  Newfoundlands 178–179
  noses 202
  Pekingeses 39
  on phone 213
  Pomeranians 61
  poodles 119, 172
  puppies 41
  rich dogs 172
  shopping 85
  singing 187
  sleep 7, 196–197
  small dogs 14–15, 151, 206
  stray dogs 186
  in suitcase 53
  sweating 188
  swimming 178–179
  tails 143
  tongues 39, 208
  tricks 119, 152, 170
  ugly dogs 200–201
  Yorkshire terriers 206
donkeys 91, 147

E
ears 9, 38–39, 100, 104, 154, 175
elephants 124, 125, 198
eyelids 58, 107
eyes 24, 94, 108, 122, 217

F
feathers 216, 217

PHOTO CREDITS

Collect them all!

Did you enjoy that?

www.ripleys.com/books